T0221735

A Life of Song

THE STORY OF ELLA JENKINS

Written by Ty-Juana Taylor

Illustrated by Jade Johnson

Ella Jenkins always had an ear for rhythm and rhyme.

Growing up in Chicago, Illinois,
she soaked up all the
sounds around her.

Ella lived with her mother, brother, Aunt Big Mama, and Uncle Flood. Every day when Uncle Flood returned home from work, Ella found her way to the dining room to watch him play one of the many harmonicas he kept in his vest.

When he played his blues tunes, Ella hummed and whistled along.

She wanted to create her own music just like Uncle Flood.
Ella found thin paper and wrapped it around a comb. She blew on it
and out came a buzzing sound. It didn't sound like the full melodies
that came from Uncle Flood's harmonica, but it was a sound she'd
created all on her own.

Ella's mother could see her baby loved to make music. Mother worked hard all day long, washing clothes, cooking food, and cleaning homes around Chicago. She saved every penny until she had enough money to buy her daughter a harmonica.

When Ella played, she found her voice. Out poured notes that she could bend with a single breath or wobble with the cup of her hand.

The harmonica opened a new world for Ella. She could do more than listen to the rhythms and sounds around her. She could make them herself!

One day, she discovered that the famous jazz musician Cab Calloway was coming to the Regal Theater. The city buzzed with excitement. Ella's brother got free tickets and invited Ella to see Cab perform.

The cool of the vast dark theater surrounded them as they settled into the soft velvet seats. Then the audience burst into applause as Cab Calloway and his band took the stage.

Cab Calloway sang,

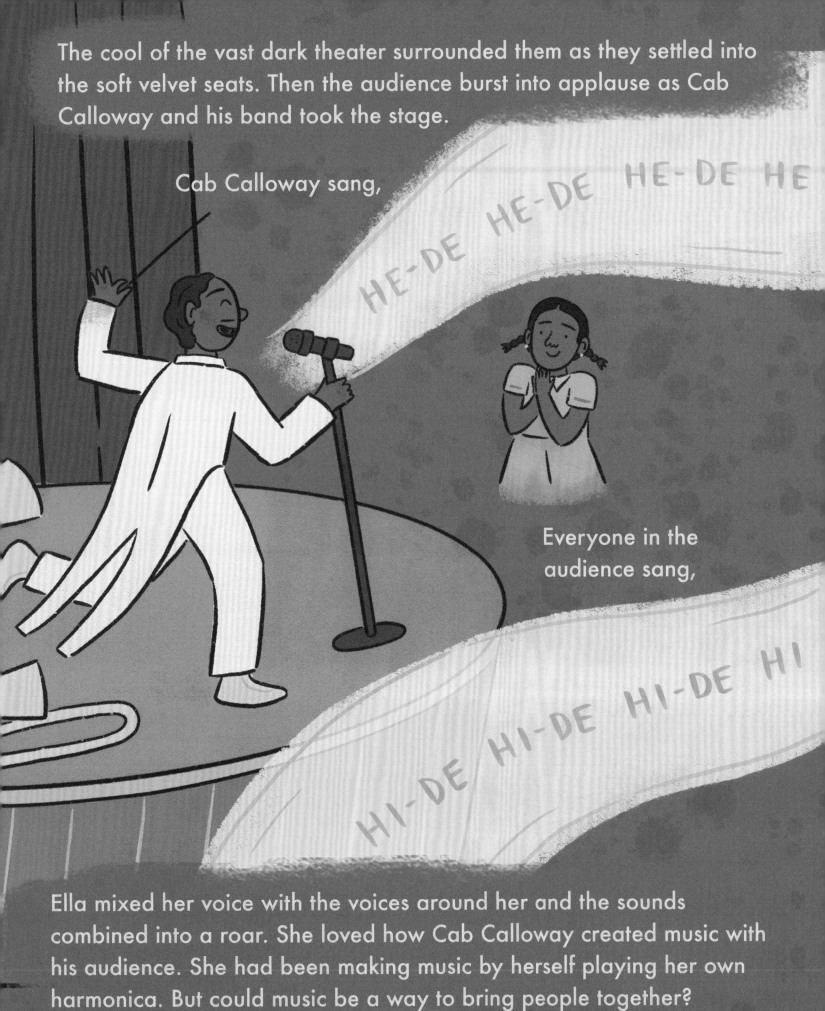

HE-DE HE-DE HE-DE HE

Everyone in the audience sang,

HI-DE HI-DE HI-DE HI

Ella mixed her voice with the voices around her and the sounds combined into a roar. She loved how Cab Calloway created music with his audience. She had been making music by herself playing her own harmonica. But could music be a way to bring people together?

Ella had reason to wonder about how to bring people together.

In the 1940s, Chicago was a segregated city where Black people could only live around Black people. They had to go to separate schools, eat in separate restaurants, and could not get the same jobs because of the color of their skin. Ella could see that "separate but equal" was not equal.

Even though people lived separated by race, Ella made friends who had different backgrounds. All of her friends shared the belief that it was wrong to treat people differently just because of the color of their skin. They supported equality and civil rights for all.

As talk about civil rights grew louder, Ella's voice grew louder too. Protests sprouted throughout the city, and she joined in.

They marched,

held sit-ins,

and boycotted to demand equality for all.

And of course, Ella sang.

CHANGE IS A-COMING

Ella realized that music could be her tool to bring people together and fight for a fair and equal world. To reach her dream, she would have to leave her home in the South Side of Chicago.

Ella moved to San Francisco for college, where she studied child psychology. She lived and worked at a Jewish girls' boarding home. The girls taught her Jewish songs and told her about Jewish culture.

Ella was hungry to learn more music. Just as she had as a child, Ella soaked up all the sounds around her.

She learned Cuban music from Cuban percussionist Armando Peraza.

She sang spirituals with Brother John Sellers.

She riffed and improvised jazz tunes with Big Bill Broonzy.

Even when Ella returned to Chicago, she continued to sing songs from different cultures. She took a job as a program director at the YWCA and introduced songs she learned to kids at the YWCA.

She'd sing,

MOON DON'T GO...

And they would echo back,

...MOON DON'T GO

Ella used Cab Calloway's call-and-response technique to create simple rhythmic songs with children.

Ella had found her path. She decided to become a professional musician. And she knew just the audience that would embrace the new rhythms and languages she had learned: children.

In 1956, she created a seven-year plan to become a professional musician. Her first step was to make a music album. Using her own instruments, she recorded four songs she'd written. A friend urged her to travel to New York to meet Moses Asch, the founder of Folkways Recordings.

Ella took the next bus to New York and boldly approached Mo with her songs.

He loved her work and her confidence. He signed her to his record label right then and there. Soon, she recorded her first album, *Call and Response: Rhythmic Group Singing*.

Just as she was creating her album, Ella was asked to teach world music on a show called "This is Rhythm" on Totem Club, a popular children's television show.

HOME

She shared American folk
songs, Japanese folk and
dance songs, and South African
children's songs. She introduced
music from around the world to
children across Chicago.
Ella also took her audience back in time to follow the rhythms and songs
that enslaved people created. She sang spirituals like "Steal Away" and
spoke about the cruelties of American slavery.

Principals saw Ella on television and began inviting her to perform for schools throughout the United States. She drove through many states, singing for children in the countryside and children in the cities.

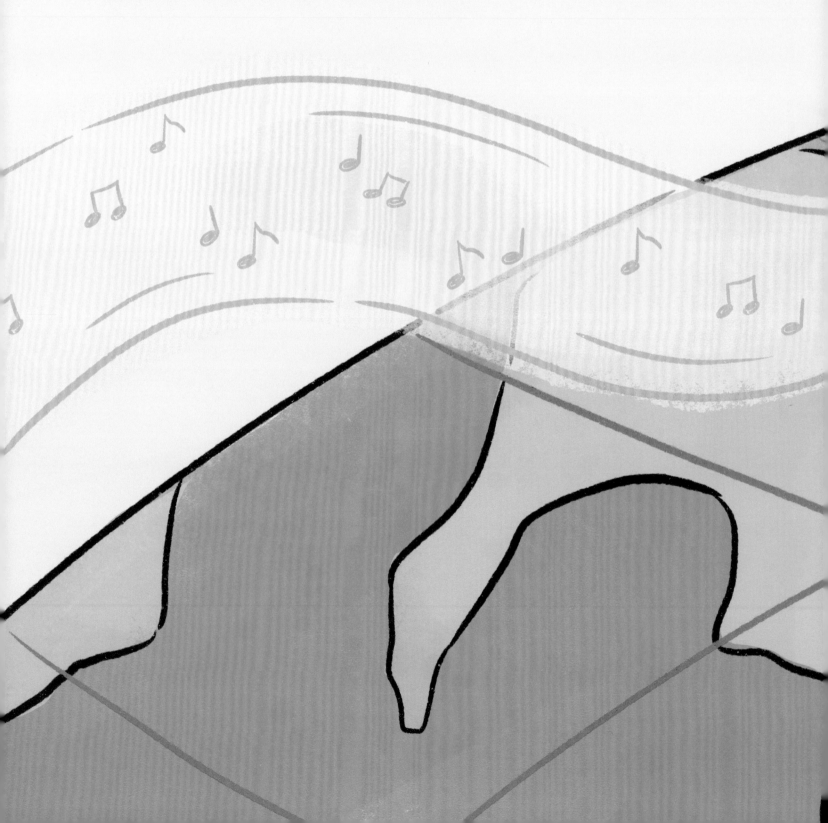

During this time, the fight for civil rights was spreading across the United States. Those who were against this change used their power, and sometimes violence, to resist this change. Even though it could be dangerous, Ella still took to the road. She brought along the only tool she needed to fight discrimination and racism: music.

Each place brought its challenges. Ella would get a terrible feeling in her stomach when she arrived somewhere new. She never knew if people would be unkind to her because of the color of her skin. Sometimes, she wasn't allowed to stay at a hotel because she was Black. In other places, restaurant owners wouldn't allow her to eat at their restaurants.

Ella stood tall and demanded to be treated as an equal. She told school principals to call the hotels and restaurants to make sure they gave her and her drivers a place to stay and eat. Ella knew she had the gift of music to offer the world.

Despite the discrimination she faced on tour, Ella loved sharing music with children because they were open-minded and curious. They were ready for new sounds, new songs, and new ideas.

Her audience participated in every performance. They clapped, jumped, danced, and sang along.

She sang,

WHO FED THE CHICKENS?

They sang,

Making music with children was a revolutionary act.
Singing together helped to tear down barriers like segregation,
which kept people apart. For many children, Ella was the first
Black woman they saw on a stage, In charge, and leading the
whole room together.

WE FED THE CHICKENS!

Ella's career continued to grow. She made many music albums and toured the world. During her travels, she learned songs from different cultures and explored these songs' lyrics and rhythms with children.

When she returned home, Ella continued to use her music to unite people.

In 1964, she performed at the Martin Luther King Jr. Illinois Rally for Civil Rights at Soldier Field. Tens of thousands of people endured the sweltering heat and rain to stand together.

A SONG TOGETHER...

Today, Ella's music can be heard in homes and classrooms across the globe.

Her courageous acts helped children connect to each other and see that they were more alike than different.

...IN WARM OR WINTRY WEATHER

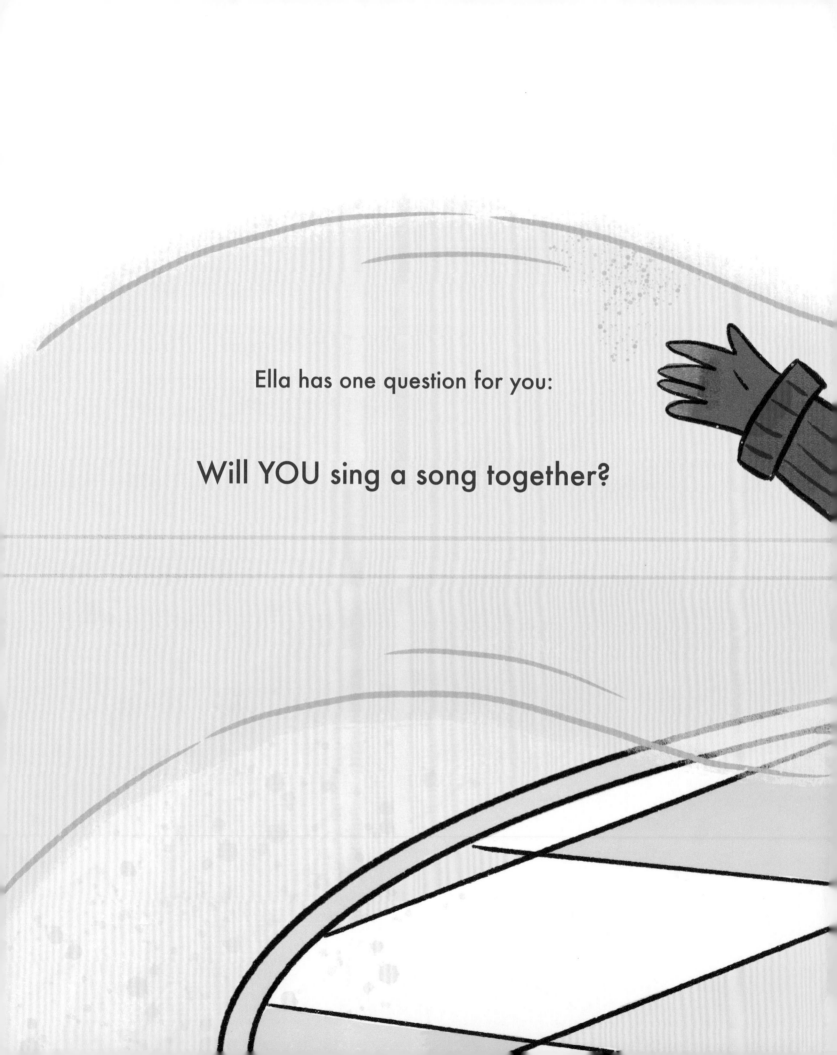

Ella has one question for you:

Will YOU sing a song together?

Ella and pre-teen rhythm-makers make a guest appearance on Chicago's popular Lee Phillip Show.

Ella shared music with children on all seven continents, in countless countries, and in all 50 states in America.

Ella shares some Latin rhythms with nursery school children in York Center Community, a residential development near Chicago.

She learned instruments like the ukulele, castanets, claves, tom-toms, bamboo drums, bongos, and güiros during her travels. Ella's music helped her connect and build bridges with people everywhere.

Ella playing her favorite conga drum.

She learned new songs wherever she went.

While touring schools in the South in the 1960s, Ella met future U.S. Representative John Lewis and learned the song, "You Better Leave Segregation Alone."

In New Zealand, she learned a Maori battle chant when she discovered that the Maori people were also fighting for their rights. In East Africa, she learned how to count in Swahili.

U.S. Representative John Lewis and Ella Jenkins at the Living Legend for Service to Humanity Award ceremony in 2011. The two first met in 1965 while he was a Freedom Rider and she was touring HBCUs.

Photo by Doreen Hines

Ella and a koala.

Just as she had as a child, Ella soaked up all the sounds around her.

Ella playing the ukulele.

Ella's music career spanned 70 years. Her work was groundbreaking in many ways.

She was one of the first musicians to tour and create music for children.

She was the first Black woman to host her own show for children in Chicago.

She was the first children's musician to be given a Grammy Lifetime Achievement Award.

She was the first children's musician to be honored as a National Endowment for the Arts National Heritage Fellow.

To Ella, Bernadelle, and Tim. You all made this story possible.
— T.T.

For my mom, grandma, and Shiki and the beats we dance to.
— J.J.

A *Life of Song: The Story of Ella Jenkins* is first published by Gloo Books 2024

Written by Ty-Juana Taylor
Illustrated by Jade Johnson

The illustrations in this book were rendered digitally.

For more information or to order books, please visit www.gloobooks.com or contact us at contact@gloobooks.com.

ISBN: 978-1-7372404-3-3
Printed in China

Follow us @gloobooks.